PROFESSIONAL GAMING CAREERS

by Sue Bradford Edwards

Norwood House Press
P.O. Box 316598
Chicago, Illinois 60631

For information regarding Norwood House Press, please visit our website at:
www.norwoodhousepress.com or call 866-565-2900.

Content Consultant: Jennifer DeWinter

LIBRARY OF CONGRESS CATALOGING-IN-PUBLICATION DATA

Names: Edwards, Sue Bradford, author.
Title: Professional gaming careers / by Sue Bradford Edwards.
Description: Chicago, Illinois : Norwood House Press, [2017] | Series:
  E-sports. game on! | Audience: Age 8-12. | Includes bibliographical
  references and index.
Identifiers: LCCN 2017004454 (print) | LCCN 2017019899 (ebook) | ISBN
  9781684041350 (eBook) | ISBN 9781599538907 (library edition : alk. paper)
Subjects: LCSH: Sports--Vocational guidance--Juvenile literature. |
  Sports--Computer network resources--Juvenile literature. | Computer
  games--Design--Vocational guidance--Juvenile literature. | Computer
  games--Programming--Vocational guidance--Juvenile literature.
Classification: LCC GV734.3 (ebook) | LCC GV734.3 .E38 2017 (print) | DDC
  796.023--dc23
LC record available at https://lccn.loc.gov/2017004454

302N—072017
Manufactured in the United States of America in North Mankato, Minnesota.

CONTENTS

Note: Words that are **bolded** in the text are defined in the glossary.

CHAPTER 1

Hackers and Early Games

Fans watch the online video **feed** as the players race through stone rooms and water-filled canals. Dennis "Thresh" Fong runs through *Quake's* Castle of the Damned map, grabbing armor and health upgrades. He watches for his opponent, Tom "Entropy" Kimzey.

When Kimzey comes into view, he gets blasted. Fong seems to know whenever he will appear. Disoriented by Fong's attack, Kimzey accidently kills himself. The final score in Red Annihilation, the first United States video game **tournament**, held in May 1997, is 14 to -1.

The Beginning

The personal computers that ran *Quake* in the 1990s far outpowered the first computers gamers used. Gaming got its start when the Digital Equipment Corporation donated a PDP-1 computer to the Massachusetts Institute of Technology (MIT) in 1961. Unlike today's computers, the PDP-1 wouldn't fit on a desk or in someone's lap. It was as big as three refrigerators. The PDP series of computers was among the first to have a keyboard and monitor so users could easily read prompts and typed commands.

The PDP-1 was the forerunner of today's gaming computers.

Hackers, a group of university students known for creating quick solutions to technical problems, looked for fun ways to use the PDP-1. They created a game called *Spacewar!*

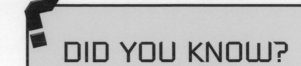

DID YOU KNOW?

Spacewar! is an open-source creation. That means how it was made is known to the public. Students with computer lab access worked on program tapes publicly stored in the MIT lab.

One hacker wrote the basic game with spaceships firing at each other. Another added a starry background, and a third introduced a gravity-heavy sun to pull ships off course. Hackers raided the school's model railroad club for parts and built game controllers. By February 1962, they had developed a basic video game.

The First Tournament

Spacewar! spread to other universities that had PDP computers. The first competition occurred when *Rolling Stone* magazine wanted to write about a tournament and

Stanford University in Palo Alto, California, was the site of the first E-Sports tournament in 1972.

sponsored the event. On October 19, 1972, the magazine sent reporter Stewart Brand and photographer Annie Leibovitz to Stanford University to cover the *Spacewar!* tournament. Twenty Stanford students and researchers crowded into the school's Artificial Intelligence Lab.

In the free-for-all, five ships dodged mines and other players' missiles. Each gamer had a unique style of play.

Bruce Baumgart emerged as the winner. The team competition was won by Slim Tovar and Robert A. Maas. Meanwhile, gamers like these were looking for ways to make gaming more popular.

Pinball machines filled arcades before video games took over in the 1970s.

Arcade Play

One *Spacewar!* player, Utah engineer Nolan Bushnell, saw possibilities in arcade play. If *Spacewar!* were built like a pinball machine, it could spread beyond university computers. He simplified the game so enemy ships were controlled by a computer chip.

Model Railways

MIT's first hackers were members of the Tech Model Railroad Club's Signals and Power Subcommittee. Model railroad clubs build working models of railroads running through towns, over mountains, and across rivers. The subcommittee maintained the electrical wires, switches, and circuits that powered the trains. Hackers looked for clever, high-tech ways to solve problems.

His arcade game, *Computer Space*, launched in 1971. It was played alongside pinball games throughout the United States. Players in video arcades competed for high scores and perfect games on *Computer Space* and other games during the 1980s and '90s. The organization Twin Galaxies began tracking video game records in 1981 and still does today.

Gaming Comes Home

With small, powerful home computers, gaming spread worldwide in the 1990s. Players accessed fast, reliable Internet and challenged each other to a range of games.

Home video game consoles brought the excitement of the arcade into the comfort of players' homes.

First came fighting games, such as *Street Fighter* and *Mortal Kombat,* with two players in hand-to-hand combat. In **first-person** shooters, including *Call of Duty* and *Halo*, one band of fighters hunts another. Games based on traditional sports included soccer and auto racing. Two players compete in real-time strategy (RTS) games such as *StarCraft I,* while teams battle in

Headsets and microphones allow players to communicate with each other from home.

DID YOU KNOW?

Online gamers play using gamer tags or screen names. Dennis Fong played as "Thresh," Johnathan Wendel as "Fatal1ty," and Matt Haag as "NaDeSHot."

Carpal Tunnel Syndrome

Carpal tunnel syndrome is a hand injury that causes tingling, numbness, and pain when a nerve is pinched in the wrist. Sometimes it is the result of an injury, but daily computer users often develop this problem. Caught early, it can often be treated with ice and frequent breaks. In serious cases, a surgeon cuts the tissue that is putting pressure on the nerve.

multiplayer online battle arenas (MOBAs) in *League of Legends* and *Dota*.

As more people gamed, tournaments offered larger prizes, and winning gamers were considered professionals. Among the first was Fong, who didn't lose a game of *Quake* or *Doom* in competition or practice from 1994 to 1996. In May 1997, he won the Red Annihilation *Quake* tournament in Atlanta, Georgia. The grand prize was $5,000 and a customized Ferrari. Fong retired after this, in part because he had **carpal tunnel** pains in his hands from gaming.

DID YOU KNOW?

Travelers need a document known as a work visa to work in another country. The US government grants professional gamers the same visa issued to professional athletes when they travel abroad to compete.

Another early pro gamer was Johnathan "Fatal1ty" Wendel. In 2000 he told his dad that if he didn't win big at his first tournament, he would quit. Instead he earned $4,000. Wendel specialized in several games, including *Quake, Counter-Strike,* and *Painkiller.* Wendel and Fong showed everyone it is possible to make a name in gaming.

What it Takes to Go Pro

No matter what they play, pro gamers share several key traits. The most important trait is they love gaming. They don't necessarily love all games or even most games, but they love the games they play. Because so many games are free, professionals recommend that new gamers try several games of each type to find games they love. It takes countless hours of practice to reach the highest ranks.

Top gamers are also **analytical**, planning out moves and anticipating what an opponent may do. Many people compare RTS and MOBA games to chess. Some professional gamers even play chess to help improve their game. *StarCraft* pro Sasha "Scarlett" Hostyn excelled at *xiangqi*, or Chinese chess, when she was only 11 years old.

Chinese chess helped Sasha Hostyn develop her analytical skills for her career as a pro gamer.

Quick reflexes and manual **dexterity** are key to making accurate moves as a pro gamer. One hand may be clicking a mouse while the other is keying in a command. Top-level *StarCraft* play can require as many as 300 actions in a single minute.

DID YOU KNOW?

All gamers are looking to win every time they play. But no one appreciates wasting precious game time. If someone is obviously going to lose, the losing gamer is expected to message "GG," for "good game," to admit defeat.

Gaming as a Family Affair

Making it as a professional takes a lot of work and motivation. Many professionals have the support of family and friends. Sasha Hostyn's father also games. He networked the family's three computers so they could play StarCraft together. Her brother Sean started playing six months before Sasha did. But she beat him within two weeks. Family participation isn't essential, but it can make gaming more fun.

Try, Try Again

In addition to certain **innate skills**, the professional gamer must develop other skills. *StarCraft* and fighting games are extremely complicated, so no new gamer excels instantly. Gamers reach the upper levels after hours of play in which they carefully learn their game controller or keyboard, which helps improve their response times. As the old saying goes, practice makes perfect. Many gamers like Hostyn travel to tournaments with their own keyboard and mouse.

Pros are also familiar with the game itself. If a gamer can choose from various characters, they need to know each character's strengths and weaknesses, attacks, and movements. To play well, they have to know what each character can do.

As with any sport, each E-sport opponent varies. Playing another gamer is very different from playing the computer. **AI**, or artificial intelligence, behaves and reacts differently than a person. Gamers play both ways for maximum skill.

Pro gamers must have expert command of the keyboard and mouse.

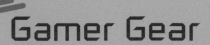

Gamer Gear

When gamers are choosing gear, some buy a PlayStation or Xbox for competition. Others go with a desktop computer they can customize to always have the current hardware. When playing as part of a team in one location, it's important to have compatible systems and knowledge of how to set up a network. Gear doesn't have to be fancy. Many gamers prefer basic mice over something with built-in acceleration. Mice with acceleration will keep speeding up the cursor as the mouse moves. Muscle memory is considered more reliable by some gamers.

Through practice, gamers learn to deal with the frustration of losing. Everyone is disappointed when they lose, but it doesn't affect the pros. If it does, they won't be ready for their next game.

Game On

Game play is what gaming is all about. Most people play best at home with friends. There they know the game, the controller, and the competition. They are in control.

Tournament play in front of thousands of fans is entirely different. Hostyn, who calls herself very **introverted**, admits

Pro gamers display maximum focus throughout a competition.

that at the beginning of her career the thought of being on
stage in front of so many people terrified her. Although she
would be playing in a booth and wearing headphones, she

DID YOU KNOW?

Today, team players wear earbuds and noise-canceling headphones. This allows them to hear each other over the noise of the crowd. At early tournaments, it wasn't uncommon for players to get sore throats from shouting to hear one another.

piped in **white noise** to make sure all the other sounds were gone.

It is hard to learn how to play well at tournaments. The best way is simply by playing in them. Pro gamers are part of gaming leagues such as Major League Gaming or ELEAGUE. Once a new gamer has joined a league, he or she needs to decide which events are a good fit. A good fit depends on the league, the game, and whether or not the gamer plays as part of a team.

Many gamers choose to wear headphones to block out as much background noise as possible while competing.

CHAPTER 3

Practice Makes Perfect

Professional gamers all have a practice **regimen**. What goes into this training program varies from gamer to gamer, but there are things that almost every gamer does.

Daily Playing Time

A big part of every regimen is game play, but the daily number of hours each gamer plays varies. South Korean professional gamers are notorious for pushing the limits. Chae "Piglet" Gwang-jin and Kim "Fenix" Jae-hun, members of the *League of Legends* Team Liquid, play from 12 to 14 hours every day. In contrast, Peter "ppd" Dager plays *Dota 2* with his teammates about 4 hours daily.

Hostyn also limits her daily play to 3 or 4 hours a day. She believes when a player games 12 hours a day, play

South Korean team SK Telecom T1 celebrates a 2013 *League of Legends* title.

becomes **rote** instead of being mindful. This can become a problem in strategic games, like *StarCraft*. She also has **tendinitis**, which can cause pain in her hand and wrist unless she limits her playing time.

Online Action

A big part of online play is seeking out people at every skill level. This is important because players need to work with people at their own skill level so that they can learn to work as part of a team. New gamers also need to play with more skilled gamers to improve their overall gaming skills.

Gamers seeking more skilled players should check rankings and not go by gamer tags. Many professional gamers prefer to play anonymously whenever possible.

Hostyn uses a **bar code**, a series of vertical lines in place of a name. It looks like the bar code that a price scanner uses to ring up purchases at the store. Many of the world's best gamers also use them.

DID YOU KNOW?

According to Dager, captain of the *Dota 2* team Evil Geniuses, E-sports fans can break into the world of professional competition if they have nimble fingers and a good brain. He says that the only other thing they need is the desire to dedicate themselves to the game.

Tendinitis

Tendinitis is a painful swelling of a tendon. A tendon is flexible tissue that attaches muscle to bone. This irritation is caused by overuse and may occur in the hand, wrist, or elbow. Hobbies, such as gaming, that involve repetitive motions are one of the most common ways people develop tendinitis. Mild tendinitis can be managed with physical therapy exercises, rest, and medication to manage pain. Severe tendinitis, when a tendon **ruptures**, requires surgery.

Professionals also study other players' games. One way to do this is by watching videos online to learn strategies that led to a win. Hostyn acknowledges that she learns almost as much this way as she does gaming.

When and Where

Pro gamers set their game times according to when other gamers can be online. Dager and his team would meet online at approximately 1:00 p.m. in the Eastern Time Zone. This allowed players from Northern California, Vancouver, and Sweden several hours of game play together per day.

Hostyn lives in Kingston, Ontario, in eastern Canada. When she goes online in the late afternoon, she looks for opponents in Europe where, because of the time difference, it is nighttime. This means that these players are online instead of being in school or at work.

Some players even relocate in order to challenge elite South Korean players, largely considered the world's best. Swedish *StarCraft* player Johan "Naniwa" Lucchesi trained in Korea in the fall of 2011. He felt it was the only way to reach the top of his game. Hostyn agrees. She lived in Korea for nearly a year. Both players claim, however, that they were very lonely in South Korea.

No two gamers have the same practice regimen. Practicing with comparable or more skilled players helps gamers sharpen their

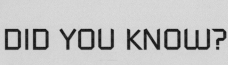

DID YOU KNOW?

Pro gamers like Hostyn often wear two sets of headphones. A pair of earbuds provides sound from the game. Headphones worn over those drown out other sounds like crowd noise.

Gamers sometimes keep odd hours to make time for practice.

skills. Studying strategy helps them learn tricks to use in their next game. Once gamers have developed the skills they need, they are ready to think about going pro.

A technology hub, South Korea is home to some of the world's best gamers.

CHAPTER 4

Tournaments and More

Although the first thing most people think about is winning cash prizes at tournaments, professional gamers make money in a variety of ways. Sponsorships and live streaming are more reliable sources of income.

Tournament Competition

Early tournaments for *Street Fighter* and *Doom* often attracted only several hundred players. The small cash prizes were seldom enough to pay for travel and hotel rooms. Marcus "djWHEAT" Graham often spent $1,000 just to win $800. Graham was a pro gamer in the 1990s but now works in the E-sports industry.

As gaming has become more popular, competitors, spectators, and prize money have all increased. In 2012,

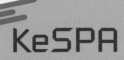

KeSPA

In 2000 South Korea formed the Korea e-Sports Association (KeSPA). It launched several E-sports leagues. Major Korean companies sponsor teams the same way they sponsor baseball teams. The gamers on these teams live and train in sponsor-provided housing. But the opportunities aren't just for gamers. In 2004 the Proleague final tournament in the coastal city of Busan attracted 100,000 spectators.

Major League Gaming's Spring Championship in Anaheim, California, paid out $200,000 in prize money. *League of Legends* teams often compete for $5 million in prizes. Although prizes have increased in size, travel expenses can still be high for US-based gamers who travel to tournaments in Europe and Asia.

While tournament payouts might look good, that money goes to only a small number of people. In November 2015, the *Hearthstone* World Championship offered a $100,000 grand prize, but that went to only one player, Sebastian "Ostkaka" Engwall. Still, there are other ways for gamers to earn income.

The Fuse team prepares for a 2014 Major League Gaming tournament.

Sponsorships

Once a gamer has a serious following, he or she can get corporate sponsors. Inviting a company to become

DID YOU KNOW?

Twitch.tv is a popular live-streaming gaming platform. Its goal is to be a safe, welcoming space for gamers of all ages. Kids ages 13 to 18 need permission from a parent or legal guardian to sign up. And in 2015, they banned games rated as "adults only" by the Entertainment Software Rating Board.

Teams vie for money, prestige, and trophies at pro gaming tournaments.

a sponsor is a lot like applying for a job. In this case, gamers have to show sponsors they have what it takes to help the sponsor make money. For the pro gamer, this means having a big social media following or many website hits.

Live Streaming Feeds

Another way to make money is to live stream, which allows fans to watch a pro play in real time. Players broadcast their practice matches and provide commentary through their webcams. Large numbers of fans mean a higher income. The income is based on advertising **revenue**. Sometimes fans make donations directly to a gamer. The more hours a gamer streams, and the more fans the gamer attracts, the higher the income generated.

Streaming provides opportunities beyond just watching professional gamers play. Fans can also ask questions and make comments in chat groups. And gamers can broadcast more than game play, too. In 2014 Chinese gamer Zhang "Xiao8" Ning streamed his wedding. The event drew 320,000 fans. Streaming offers new ways for fans and gamers to connect and share.

Live streaming, sponsorships, and tournament earnings can combine to make a good living for talented gamers who are committed to serious play. The best can earn up to $100,000 per year just from live streaming.

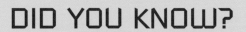

DID YOU KNOW?

The gaming market reached about $107 billion in 2017. This dollar total includes the money spent on video games, computers, and various game systems. That put it just ahead of the film industry on the list of biggest entertainment markets.

CHAPTER 5

Gaming Today and Tomorrow

Who is considered a top gamer varies based on the **criteria** used for evaluation. If it is based on career earnings, the players on team Newbee rank high on the list. In 2014 they won Valve's *Dota 2* tournament in Seattle, Washington. The grand prize, just over $5 million, made Chen "Hao" Zhihao, Zhang "Mu" Pan, Zhang "Xiao8" Ning, Zhou "KingJ" Yang, and Gong "ZSMJ" Jian instant millionaires.

Other gamers are known for their social media presence. Matt "NaDeSHot" Haag plays on the team Optic Gaming. In addition to making more than $1 million a year, Haag has more than one million social media followers. Haag's streaming sessions give fans a peek into his life while he discusses midnight snacks and more.

Members of Newbee compete in a *Dota 2* match in Shanghai, China, in 2014.

Still other gamers are making history. In 2015, Kayla "Squizzay" Squires, part of the team Pure N3gs, was the first female player to qualify for the *Call of Duty* World

Getting in the Game

E-sports continues to evolve into a spectator sport. An update to *Dota 2* in 2016 made it easier for fans to not only watch, but also to feel a part of the game. Virtual reality enables viewers to transport themselves onto the battlefield. There they can watch the action unfold around them. The technology made its debut at The International tournament in August.

League. Long-time E-sports reporter Rod Breslau tweeted about her historic achievement. He noted how huge it was for women in E-sports. Squires had proved that women were among the world's best gamers.

Women in Gaming

Squires's win was a big deal because most professional gamers are male. Some gamers believe that enthusiastic women often quit playing because of bad experiences.

Two researchers, Michael Kasumovic of the University of New South Wales and Jeffrey Kuznekoff of Miami University, studied *Halo 3* gamers. They chose this game because players are assigned randomly to teams and the heavily armored **avatars** aren't gender specific. The only clue to a gamer's gender is his or her voice. They found that losing male gamers were

More and more women are participating in E-Sports every year.

Lisette Sheikh plays a *Counter-Strike: Global Offensive* match at the 2015 Dreamhack Gaming Convention.

often hostile to players who sounded female. In contrast, skilled male gamers didn't harass female gamers.

Many women say this **harassment** is why they join all-female teams. They feel women offer more support.

Gold Medal Gamers?

E-sports can already make a gamer rich. Someday they could make gamers the pride of their country. In 2016 South Korea's International e-Sports Federation took their first steps toward making E-sports an Olympic sport. If approved, E-sports could make their Olympic debut in Tokyo in 2020.

They also think female teams show that there is a place for women in the world of gaming.

By the summer of 2016, all-women tournaments were popping up around the world. SKYLLA is a European *Counter-Strike: Global Offensive* tournament. It encourages women to play alongside

DID YOU KNOW?

The youngest player to earn $1 million in E-sports is Sumail Hassan Syed from Pakistan. He was 16 years, 2 months, and 21 days old when he won The International in 2015. His career earnings to that point were $1,639,867.

Virtual reality technology immerses players in the game.

male players. The goal of SKYLLA is to promote a gaming environment welcoming to both men and women.

Gaming Tomorrow

From *Spacewar!* to *StarCraft*, gamers have a different experience now than they had 50 years ago. Just how gaming will change in the next 50 years will depend on emerging technology.

The way games are played will also change. One gaming insider predicts that the keyboard and mouse will be replaced, perhaps by touchscreen technology. Games are already played on iPhones and tablets, so it is only a matter of time before a touchscreen-based game attracts serious gamers.

Other possible upgrades include motion sensors, eye movement tracking sensors, virtual reality in the form of goggles or helmets, and more. E-sports is an exciting, constantly changing industry. The only certain thing about the future is the thrilling innovations that inevitably lie ahead for tomorrow's pro gamers.

DID YOU KNOW?

Some colleges offer gaming scholarships. Chicago's Robert Morris University offers *League of Legends* players an annual scholarship worth up to $19,000.

GLOSSARY

AI

Artificial intelligence. A computer's ability to perform operations in a manner similar to decision-making and learning in humans.

analytical

Able to analyze information and think logically, often planning out a strategy.

avatars

Images that represent players or characters in a game.

bar code

A series of vertical lines that contains information when scanned.

carpal tunnel

A painful hand and wrist injury caused by overuse.

criteria

A set of rules used to evaluate or define something.

dexterity

Skill and ability in using the hands or body.

feed

A radio, television, or Internet broadcast.

first-person

In E-sports, gameplay that proceeds from the perspective of the player.

hackers

People who are highly skilled in computers or electronics and use them in creative ways.

harassment

The act of repeatedly attacking someone by saying harsh and hateful things.

innate skills

Abilities a person has from birth.

introverted

A reserved or shy person.

regimen

Repeated exercises meant to build skill at a task or set of tasks.

revenue

Money or earnings.

rote

Doing things in a mechanical, routine way.

ruptures

Breaks or bursts open.

tendinitis

A painful swelling of a tendon.

tournament

A series of contests that tests players' skills.

white noise

Steady, unchanging sound used to drown out other noises.

Books

Guinness World Records 2017 Gamer's Edition. London: Guinness World Records, 2017.

Kaplan, Arie. *The Epic Evolution of Video Games.* Minneapolis, MN: Lerner Publications Company, 2014.

Paris, David and Stephanie. *History of Video Games.* Huntington Beach, CA: Teacher Created Materials, 2016.

Roesler, Jill. *Online Gaming: 12 Things You Need to Know.* North Mankato, MN: 12-Story Library, 2016.

Websites

Eleague Official Website

www.eleague.com

Evil Geniuses Team Site

www.evilgeniuses.gg

Major League Gaming

www.majorleaguegaming.com

Team Liquid

www.teamliquidpro.com

INDEX

Sue Bradford Edwards is a Missouri nonfiction author who writes about science, culture, and history. Her books about science and computers include *Women in Science* and *Hidden Human Computers: The Black Women of NASA*. When she isn't working, she games with her teen son although she's not nearly as good as he is.